T0193845

HOW TO TEACH
LITERATURE

INTRODUCTORY COURSE

STUDENT REVIEW
QUESTIONS AND TESTS

ELIZABETH MCCALLUM MARLOW

WESTBOW
PRESS®
A DIVISION OF THOMAS NELSON
& ZONDERVAN

WestBow Press books may be ordered through booksellers or by contacting:

WestBow Press
A Division of Thomas Nelson & Zondervan
1663 Liberty Drive
Bloomington, IN 47403
www.westbowpress.com
1 (866) 928-1240

ISBN: 978-1-9736-5853-5 (sc)
ISBN: 978-1-9736-5852-8 (e)

Print information available on the last page.

WestBow Press rev. date: 3/29/2019

To the Teacher

The following review questions and tests are designed to be used in conjunction with *How to Teach Literature: Introductory Course*. All review questions and tests are included in the teaching guide and reproduced in this booklet with answers omitted.

Review questions

Copy and distribute a set of review questions to your class. Students break into small groups and refer to their literature books and notes as each group answers the questions. Every student answers the questions in his or her notebook. On an assigned day, students hand in their notebooks with the completed questions for grading. At a later date, the teacher should review with the class appropriate answers to each set of review questions. The teacher may choose to use some of the questions on tests and semester exams.

Tests

Test procedure[1]

A. Taking tests[2]

Have students clear their desks and take out a pen. Distribute tests. Require students to place a cover sheet on top of their tests and move it down to cover answers as they take the test. The teacher may also wish to arrange students' desks at some distance apart. Instruct students to use the back of the test if they require more space for their responses. As students finish a test, they should place it face down on their desks and work on other assignments until everyone has completed the test. Collect the tests.

B. Reviewing tests

Distribute graded tests and review answers. While grading the tests, the teacher may opt to note down excellent responses and ask individual students to read those responses to the class. Take time to answer students' questions about both questions and responses.

---

[1] I have found the following procedures to be effective. Other teachers may prefer to adopt methods that are more suited to the needs of a particular class.

[2] Some tests require the teacher to copy certain excerpts or poems and attach them to the back of the test.

Literature holds up a mirror to life and in so doing allows us to better understand ourselves and others.

Contents

Review questions on the Short Story Unit

Name _____

"Through the Tunnel"

1. Briefly describe the two settings in "Through the Tunnel." In your response, refer to the colors that describe both settings. What do the colors describing both settings suggest?

2. How do the two settings suggest Jerry's conflict?

3. Briefly describe the relationship between Jerry and his mother. Does it change by the end of the story?

"To Build a Fire"

4. As precisely as possible, state the setting of "To Build a Fire."

5. Who or what is the antagonist in this story?

6. List aspects of the man's personality that contribute to his death.

7. What precautions should the man have taken to ensure that he was successful in building a fire?

8. What else should the man have done to increase his chance of survival?

9. How do we know that the dog has a better instinct for survival than the man?

10. In your opinion, what is this story's climax?

"Top Man"

11. What is the setting of "Top Man?

12. Explain how the setting provides the story's conflict.

13. Apart from their nationalities, list several differences between the two protagonists.

14. In your opinion, who is "top man"? Explain your choice.

"Antaeus"

15. Explain the allusion in the title of Borden Deal's story. How does the allusion apply to T.J.?

16. What is the essential difference between T.J. and the city boys?

17. Explain why T.J. is a good leader.

"A Christmas Memory"

18. List methods of indirect characterization the author uses to convey the woman's personality.

19. What main aspects of the woman's personality are conveyed via lists?

20. What do the kites in the final paragraph symbolize?

"Thank you, M'am"

21. What is your opinion of Mrs. Jones in "Thank you, M'am"?

22. Why does Mrs. Jones tell Roger that she has done things she's ashamed of?

23. What main method of indirect characterization does Langston Hughes use to convey Mrs. Jones's personality?

"The Storm"

24. Characterization is not a key element in this story; however, we learn something about the husband and the wife's personalities. List several character traits that define each of them.

25. How does Janet's attitude to the storm change?

"The Story-Teller"

26. Identify this story's setting. Why is this particular setting indispensable to the meaning?

27. Why is the bachelor a better storyteller than the aunt?

28. Why is the theme of the bachelor's story unconventional?

29. What is ironic about Bertha's death?

"The Bridge"

30. In terms of Kostya's personality, explain why "The Bridge" is a rite of passage story.

31. You may remember that we recognize a story's theme by observing what the protagonist learns throughout the events described. Write out a one-sentence theme for this story.

"The Ransom of Red Chief"

32. What type of irony is involved in the story entitled "The Ransom of Red Chief"?

33. Explain the story's central irony.

34. List other ironies in this tale.

"The Necklace"

35. Drawing from details in the story, explain your opinion of Madame Loisel.

36. What is your opinion of Monsieur Loisel?

37. What lesson does this story teach?

"The Sniper

38. Summarize what you know about the historical background of "The Sniper."

39. What type of irony is involved in this story? Explain.

"The Open Window"

40. From what point of view is this story mainly told? Explain how we can recognize the point of view.

41. What point of view does the author adopt in the last few paragraphs? Why is the switch effective?

42. What does Mr. Nuttel assume when the three hunters come through the open window?

"The Cask of Amontillado"

43. List several examples of dramatic irony in Poe's horror story "The Cask of Amontillado."

44. List several examples of verbal irony.

45. Is Poe's narrator reliable or not? Explain.

"The Hat"

46. What is the point of view adopted in "The Hat"?

47. How can you identify this point of view?

48. State one or two of Cress's main personality traits.

Review questions on *Fahrenheit 451*

Name _____

1. Why is the title of this book appropriate?

2. How and why are the people in the world of this book controlled?

3. Provide some adjectives that describe Clarisse McClellan's family.

4. Why is Clarisse important to Guy Montag's change of character?

5. Briefly describe the Mechanical Hound. What is its function?

6. In what way is the woman who owns leather-bound books like the sixteenth-century martyrs, Bishops Latimer and Ridley?

7. What is the function of the fire chief, Captain Beatty, in this novel? What is Beatty's opinion of Montag?

8. Why is Montag's alleged death televised?

9. What is Granger's function?

10. What does the novel imply about education?

11. What does Bradbury's book have to say about history?

12. What does the book imply about parenting in the world Bradbury describes?

13. What important insight or insights have you gained from reading *Fahrenheit 451*?

Review questions on *Animal Farm*

Name _____

1. Mention some facts you have learned about the author of this novel. Include the reason why he wrote *Animal Farm*.

2. Why does Old Major call man the enemy of all animals?

3. Define these terms and apply them to the novel: fable, satire, allegory.

4. Define the main character traits of these animals: Mollie, Boxer, Clover, Benjamin.

5. What point is Orwell making by giving some animals specific character traits?

6. In *Animal Farm*, Orwell makes the same point about education as Bradbury does in *Fahrenheit 451*. Explain.

7. Define this term: propaganda.

8. Name some examples of propaganda used in this novel.

9. What is Squealer's function?

10. Name the people in Russian history that these animals represent: Old Major, Mr. Jones, Napoleon, Napoleon's puppies.

11. What do the Seven Commandments represent?

12. Define this term: revisionist history.

13. Referring to Snowball, give some examples of the way the animals' history is revised.

14. Why do the pigs allow Moses to remain at the farm?

15. What does the windmill symbolize?

16. Is there a clear protagonist and antagonist in *Animal Farm*?

17. What is Orwell's main concern in this novel?

Review questions on *Romeo and Juliet*

Name _____

1. Why do you think Shakespeare includes Rosaline in this play?

2. List the main character traits of these young men: Benvolio, Mercutio, Tybalt.

3. In what ways is Benvolio a good friend to Romeo?

4. How do Mercutio and Romeo differ in their attitudes to love?

5. Both the Nurse and the Friar could have averted the young lovers' deaths. Explain how they should have acted differently.

6. Apart from Mercutio, name another character who is Romeo's foil, and explain why he is a foil character.

7. Reread the following passage and state its purpose:
   . . . my mind misgives
   Some consequence yet hanging in the stars
   Shall bitterly begin his fearful date
   With this night's revels and expire the term
   Of a despisèd life, closed in my breast,
   By some vile forfeit of untimely death.

8. Reread Romeo's lines spoken to the Friar and state the device Shakespeare uses here:
Do thou but close our hands with holy words,
Then love-devouring death do what he dare—
It is enough I may but call her mine.

9. What is ironic about the Friar's reason for marrying the lovers?

10. What is Romeo's punishment for killing Tybalt?

11. Mention some ways in which the lovers' personalities are different.

12. When Juliet discovers Romeo's punishment, she weeps. Her mother responds: "Evermore weeping for your cousin's death?" Lady Capulet's comment is an example of _____ (complete the sentence).

13. What is this play's turning point? Explain why this event is indeed the turning point.

14. Give a valid reason for Shakespeare's making Act IV exclusively Juliet's Act.

15. Lord Capulet moves the date of Juliet's marriage to Count Paris closer by one day. Why is this decision fatal to the lovers?

16. Name several reasons why Juliet is reluctant to drink the drug the Friar has given her.

17. Are the Capulets villains or are they bad parents? Explain your opinion.

18. List several of the play's coincidences.

19. Why is it generally more satisfying to read or watch a play in which human error plays a larger role than coincidence as events unfold?

20. What is the cause of Lady Montague's death?

21. At the end of the play, how are Lord Capulet and Lord Montague reconciled?

22. In your opinion, which moment is the play's climax?

23. Do you think Romeo or Juliet is the more convincing character? Explain.

24. What action should the lovers should have taken that would probably have averted their tragic deaths?

25. Briefly state why you think future 9th grade students should study this play.

Review questions on the *Odyssey*

Name _____

1. Write out a one-sentence definition of an epic.

2. In some detail, explain why it is true to say that the *Odyssey* begins *in medias res.*

3. Like other epic poets, Homer begins his epic with a/ an _____. Supply one word and define it.

4. Does Homer blame Odysseus for the deaths of all his sailors at the hands of the sun god? Why or why not? In your response, name the sun god.

5. We mentioned that Greek boys learned about their culture by studying ancient epics. One convention was the importance of hospitality. List several examples of Homer's emphasis on hospitality in this epic.

6. What information does the *Odyssey* convey about the role of women in ancient Greek society?

7. How does Penelope extricate herself from marrying one of the suitors?

8. Why does Odysseus take ten years to sail the fairly short distance from Troy home to Ithaca?

9. Why is it fortunate that Odysseus lands on the shore of Scheria, the land of the Phaeacians?

10. Odysseus is said to be a "man skilled in all ways of contending." List some examples of the hero's ingenuity.

11. The hero is also boastful. Provide one example of an episode when his hubris is almost fatal.

12. Epic poets often used epithets for variety. Whom or what are the following epithets describing:
"the grey-eyed goddess"
"father of us all" and "the cloud-gatherer"
"the Wayfinder"
"finger tips of rose"
"the iron queen"

13. Who are the Sirens?

14. Mention two people Odysseus meets in Hades.

15. Identify these characters: Eurycleia, Argos, Antinous, and Laertes.

16. How is Penelope finally convinced that the stranger who has arrived in Ithaca is indeed her husband?

17. Why is it important that the king returns to Ithaca dressed as a beggar?

18. List the men who help Odysseus defeat the angry suitors.

19. When the relatives of the dead suitors arrive at the palace to avenge their loved ones' deaths, who ends the fighting and how does he or she do so?

20. Several words from this epic have become part of our everyday vocabulary. Define the following words as they are used today: a muse, nectar, an odyssey, a mentor.

Review questions on the poetry unit

Name _____

1 – 10: Name the poetic device or devices used in the following lines.

You may choose from these devices. You will need to use some terms more than once:
simile   metaphor   onomatopoeia   alliteration   apostrophe   personification

1. He clasps the crag with crooked hands

2. The wrinkled sea beneath him crawls

3. And like a thunderbolt he falls

4. O wild West Wind, thou breath of Autumn's being....

5. She dwelt among the untrodden ways....
    A violet by the mossy stone
    Half hidden from the eye!

6. Thou wast not born for death, immortal Bird!

7. Fair as a star, when only one
    Is shining in the sky.

8. Blow, blow thou winter wind.
   Thou art no so unkind
   As man's ingratitude.

9. Tossing their heads in sprightly dance.

10. Hear the sledges [sleighs] with the bells—
    Silver bells!
    What a world of merriment their melody foretells!
    How they tinkle, tinkle, tinkle,
    In the icy air of night!
    While the stars that oversprinkle
    All the heavens, seem to twinkle
    With a crystalline delight….

11. Mention two or three questions to ask of any poem.

12 – 14: Identify the poetic device or devices that is/are used in these lines:

12. Once upon a midnight dreary, while I pondered, weak and weary…
    While I nodded, nearly napping, suddenly there came a tapping,
    As of someone gently rapping, rapping at my chamber door….

13. Hark, hark!
    Bow-wow.
    The watch-dogs bark!

14. For the moon never beams, without bring me dreams
    Of the beautiful Annabel lee;
    And the stars never rise, but I feel the bright eyes
    Of the beautiful Annabel Lee....

15 – 21: Define these terms:

15. onomatopoeia

16. personification

17. meter

18. free verse

19. internal rhyme

20. tone

21. apostrophe

22 – 26: Identify the type of imagery in the following lines:

22. I will arise and go now, and go to Innisfree,
    And a small cabin build there, of clay and wattles [twigs] made:
    Nine bean-rows will I have there, a hive for the honeybee….

23. While I nodded, nearly napping, suddenly there came a tapping,
    As of someone gently rapping, rapping at my chamber door….

24. Little Lamb, who made thee? …
    Gave thee life, and bid thee feed…
    Gave thee clothing of delight,
    Softest clothing, woolly, bright….

25. When roasted crabs hiss in the bowl,
    Then nightly sings the staring owl,
    "Tu-whit, tu-who"
    A merry note….

26. Couched in his kennel, like a log,
    With paws of silver sleeps the dog;
    From their shadowy cote [shelter] the white breasts peep
    Of doves in a silver-feathered sleep….

Short Story Unit Test

Name _____

Your responses should be as detailed as possible.

"Through the Tunnel"

1. Do you think Jerry acted wisely? Why or why not?

2. Explain why this is a rite of passage story.

3. How does the author use contrasted settings to convey boy's dilemma?

"A Christmas Memory"

4. Describe the personality of the boy's friend. Suggest both positive and negative traits.

5. What does the writer imply with the references to kites at the end of the story?

"Thank you, M'am"

6. What is Roger's reaction to Mrs. Jones's kindness? Do you think the boy will change his behavior in future?

7. Do you think Roger is a chronic thief? Why or why not?

"Top Man"

8. Explain how the setting is the story's antagonist.

9. What do you think Nace's axe symbolizes? Explain your opinion.

"Antaeus"

10. Explain the title's connection to this story.

11. What is the role of the antagonist or antagonists in this story?

"The Bridge"

12. Explain how this story conveys a rite of passage.

13. Explain the connection between the title and the story that follows.

"The Cask of Amontillado"

14. As precisely as possible, state this story's setting.

15. Explain what we can deduce about the person to whom the narrator is speaking? Name the narrator.

16. List at least four of the story's ironies.

17. From what point of view is this story told? Why is this an effective perspective?

"The Necklace"

18. Does the author appear to be critical only of Madame Loisel? Explain your opinion.

19. Summarize some of the story's ironies.

20. What do you think the necklace symbolizes?

"The Sniper"

21. Explain in as much detail as possible the setting of this story.

22. How does the author gain our sympathy for the sniper?

"The Open Window"

23. Supply two adjectives that define the personality of Mrs. Sappleton's niece.

24. Why does the niece tell such an outrageous story to Mr. Nuttel?

25. Why do we accept the fact that Mr. Nuttel believed the girl's inventive tale?

26. Identify the change in perspective at the end of the story. Why do you think the writer changes the perspective at this point?

"To Build a Fire"

27. What is the story's conflict?

28. Why does the author include a dog in this story?

29. List as many of the man's mistakes as possible.

"The Story-Teller"

30. What is the author criticizing in this story? What do you think about his criticism?

31. Why do the children highly approve of the bachelor's story and disapprove of their aunt's ability as a storyteller?

32. What is the aunt's attitude to the bachelor's story?

"The Ransom of Red Chief"

33. In some detail explain why this story is ironic.

34. Describe the personality of "Red Chief."

35. What moment do you think is the story's climax?

36. How does O. Henry foreshadow the ending?

"The Storm"

37. In your opinion, what probably happens after Janet runs out into the storm? Explain your opinion.

38. In a short paragraph, explain how one of the stories we read has increased, to some degree, your understanding of life or human nature. Provide the title of the story in your response. Do not repeat information you have provided in your responses to other questions on this test.

Fahrenheit 451 Test

Name _____

Your responses should be specific and supported by details from the novel.

1. In as much detail as possible, explain why the firemen in Bradbury's fictitious world burn books.

2. What is the function of television screens in every home?

3. When the fire department destroys a woman's books, the woman apparently quotes Bishop Latimer who is speaking to Bishop Ridley, both famous sixteenth-century English martyrs who wanted to spread the Protestant religion throughout England. Explain the significance of the quotation.

4. Clarisse is a foil for Mildred. In some detail, contrast the personalities and values of the two women.

5. What does the fire chief attempt to tell Montag about books? Mention his name.

6. What is Mildred's attitude to Montag's reading aloud to her?

7. Faber tells Montag that books should have value and convey wisdom about life and that people should have the leisure to enjoy books. Identify Faber and his circumstances. Explain what you think about his criteria for books.

8. On the subway, Montag remembers being at the seaside as a child and trying to fill a sieve with sand. What is the point of this memory and why does he weep?

9. Why are Mildred's friends angry and distressed when Montag reads them Matthew Arnold's poem "Dover Beach"?

10. Explain the point of Faber's allusion to the Antaeus myth.

11. Briefly describe Montag's last image of Mildred.

12. Explain what Bradbury implies about censorship in this novel.

Animal Farm Test

Name _____

Your responses should be specific and supported by details from the novel.

1. Explain how Orwell provides a version of society in miniature in the characters of farm animals such as Molly, Clover, and Boxer. Why does he do so?

2. What is the function of Moses the raven? Why do the pigs allow the raven to remain at the farm?

3 –7: In terms of Orwell's allegory of Russian history whom do the following characters represent?

3. Napoleon

4. Mr. Jones

5. Old Major

6. Squealer

7. the other farm animals

8. Do you think the book has a hero or heroine? Explain.

9. How do the pigs control the other farm animals?

10. What is the significance of the pigs' decision to teach themselves, but not the other animals, to read and write?

11. Why does Squealer tell the other animals that Boxer was driven to a hospitable?

12. At the banquet at the end of the novel, Napoleon announces several changes that will take place. Which is the most significant change and why it is so important?

13. In the final scene, what transformation do the animals notice as they peer though the farmhouse windows? Why is this transformation significant?

14. This novel is filled with many instances of the animals' gullibility, and the pigs take advantage of this weakness in order to maintain control. What point is Orwell making about human behavior in the face of tyranny? What does Orwell suggest men should do in order to avoid becoming enslaved by tyrants?

15. In your opinion, what is the novel's climax? Explain.

16. One film version changes the novel's ending to make it happy. Napoleon is expelled, and the animals live happily ever afterwards. Explain whether or not you think this is a better ending than the one Orwell provided.

Romeo and Juliet Poetry Devices Test

Name _____

Identify the poetry devices used in these passages. Choose from the following list, and use each term only ONCE:

metaphor   oxymoron   allusion   dramatic irony   apostrophe

simile   pun   soliloquy   personification   foreshadowing

1. When Juliet lies in a drug-induced coma, Lord Capulet describes his apparently dead daughter:
    Death lies on her like an untimely frost
    Upon the sweetest flower of all the field. _____

2. When Mercutio suggests to his sad friend that Romeo should dance at the Capulets' party, Romeo replies,
    You have dancing shoes
    With nimble soles; I have a soul of lead
    So stakes me to the ground I cannot move. _____

3. When the lovers say goodnight after their conversation in the Capulets' orchard, Juliet cries,
    Yet I should kill thee with much cherishing....
    Parting is such sweet sorrow.... _____

4. When a major character in a play makes a long speech that reveals his thoughts, that speech is called a/an _____

5. Juliet calls out to the night:
    Come, civil night.... _____

6. Having married Juliet, Romeo awakes at dawn and says,
   Night's candles are burnt out, and jocund day
   Stands tiptoe on the misty mountain tops. _____

7. After Romeo is banished from Verona, Lady Capulet finds Juliet crying and comments,
   Ever more weeping for your cousin's death? _____

8. On his way to the Capulets' ball, Romeo comments,
   My mind misgives
   Some consequence yet hanging in the stars
   Shall bitterly begin his fearful date
   With this night's revels and expire the term
   Of a despisèd life, closed in my breast,   .
   By some vile forfeit of untimely death. _____

9. After marrying Romeo, Juliet longs for the night so that she can be united with her husband:
   Gallop apace, you fiery-footed steeds,
   Towards Phoebus' lodging! Such a wagoner
   As Phaethon would whip you to the west
   And bring in cloudy night immediately. _____

10. Underneath Juliet's balcony, Romeo cries,
    What light through yonder window breaks?
    It is the East, and Juliet is the sun! _____

Romeo and Juliet Test

Name _____

Your responses should be as detailed as possible.

1. Occasionally, Shakespeare uses rhyming couplets or prose in his dramas, but what <u>main</u> poetic form does he use in this play and all his dramas?

2. What is meant by "the Wooden O"?

3. Why are Romeo and Juliet called "star-crossed lovers"?

4. Although Rosaline never appears, what purpose does she serve by being a character in the play?

5. Why would you be glad to have a friend like Benvolio? Explain your response.

6. Most of the time, the two lovers act impulsively and unwisely. Pretend you are Romeo (boys) or Juliet (girls). List several things you would have done differently if you were faced with his or her situation. Answer this question in one full paragraph.

7. Explain why the Friar's reason for marrying the lovers is ironic.

8. Mention one or two instances of comic relief in this tragic story.

9. Explain the difference between Romeo and Mercutio's attitudes to love.

10. Explain in detail why both lovers' closest confidants are, in fact, very poor friends.

11. List ways in which Romeo and Juliet's personalities differ radically.

12. Why do you think Shakespeare gave Juliet another suitor? Suggest a logical reason or reasons for his being a character in the play.

13. Provide a reason why the following idea is a major theme in this play: A world that is full of hatred can ruin people's lives.

14. Do you think it was primarily coincidence OR human error that caused the lovers' deaths? Refer in detail to the play to support your opinion about <u>one</u> of these topics. Supply a detailed list of points.

15–25: Identify the following passages as examples of these terms:

pun, allusion, metaphor, personification, simile

You will need to use each term <u>at least once</u> and, in some cases, <u>more than once</u>.

15. Romeo to Juliet's apparent corpse:
          Shall I believe
That unsubstantial Death is amorous,
And that the lean abhorrèd monster keeps
Thee here in dark to be his paramour? _____

16. Romeo:
    Love goes toward love as schoolboys from their books. _____

17. Romeo:
    Give me a torch. I am not for this ambling.
    Being but heavy I will bear the light. _____

18. Friar:
    The gray-eyed morn smiles on the frowning night. _____

19. Juliet:
    I would tear the cave where Echo lies. _____

20. Juliet to Romeo:
    This love
    May prove a beauteous flower when next we meet. _____

21. Mercutio:
    Ask for me tomorrow, and you shall find me a grave man. _____

22. Nurse (referring to the Count then Romeo):
    I think it best you married with the county.
    O, he's a lovely gentleman!
    Romeo's a dishclout [dishcloth] to him. _____

23. Romeo:

    It seems she hangs upon the cheek of night

    As a rich jewel in an Ethiopian's ear. _____

24. Lord Capulet:

    . . . well appareled April on the heel

    Of limping winter treads. _____

25. Romeo:

    O, speak again, bright angel, for thou art

    As glorious to this night…

    As is a wingèd messenger of heaven. _____

the *Odyssey* Test

Name _____

Your responses should be as detailed as possible.

1. What is Odysseus's most outstanding character trait? In a full paragraph, describe one occasion when this trait is particularly evident.

2 – 8. Briefly identify these characters:

2. Menelaus

3. Scylla

4. Hermes

5. Nestor

6. Anticleia

7. Charybdis

8. Circe

9. Complete this sentence by supplying two names:

_____ sends the hero to Hades in order to hear from _____
who will relate what will happen to him in the future.

10. Although Odysseus is an epic hero, he is prone to error. Mention one example of a serious mistake he makes and explain his error.

11. Disguise is a motif many writers employ. Mention <u>two</u> instances of disguise in the *Odyssey.*

12 – 13: Describe the following creatures that Odysseus meets during his voyage home:

12. the Lotus Eaters

13. the Sirens

14. How does Odysseus satisfy his renowned curiosity about the Lotus Eaters and the Sirens, and how does he escape from both of those dangers?

15 – 17: Define the following words that are derived from the epic:

15. a mentor

16. a muse

17. an odyssey

18. Summarize what you have learned about ancient Greeks' attitude to hospitality.

19. Give a valid reason for Homer's including the Argos incident. Identify Argos.

20. What was the importance of the gods in Homer's time?

21. How does Telemachus mature during the course of the *Odyssey*?

22 – 23: Mention <u>two</u> examples of dramatic irony in this epic.

24. Summarize how Odysseus restores order to his kingdom.

25. Works of literature are considered to be classic if they are relevant to all cultures and time periods. List some reasons why people throughout the world continue to read Homer's epic.

Poetry Unit Test

Name _____

Imagery

1 – 5: Images appeal to one or more of our senses. Identify the sense—hearing, sight, touch, taste, or smell—that the following passages appeal to:

1. A narrow Fellow in the Grass
    Occasionally rides—
    You may have met Him—did you not
    His notice sudden is….
    (from "A narrow Fellow in the Grass," Emily Dickinson)

2. Beat! Beat! Drums! —blow! bugles! blow!
    Over the traffic of cities—over the rumble
    of wheels in the streets….
    (from "Beat! Beat! Drums!" Walt Whitman)

3. The sun that brief December day
    Rose cheerless over hills of gray….
    (from *Snow-Bound*, John Greenleaf Whittier)

4. When all aloud the wind doth blow
    And coughing drowns the parson's saw [voice]….
    When roasted crabs [crabapples] hiss in the bowl,
    Then nightly sings the staring owl….
    (from *Love's Labor's Lost*, Shakespeare)

5. Upon her hearthstone a great fire blazing
   Scented the farthest shores with cedar smoke
   And smoke of thyme….
   (from the *Odyssey*, Homer)

Personification

6 – 9: Name who or what is personified in the following lines. Then underline the words that convey the personification:

6. A wrinkled, crabbed man they picture thee,
   Old Winter, with a rugged beard as gray
   As the long moss upon the apple tree;
   Blue lipped, an ice drop at thy sharp blue nose….
   (from "A wrinkled, crabbed man they picture thee," Robert Southey)

7. Blow, blow, thou winter wind.
   Thou art not so unkind
   As man's ingratitude.
   Thy tooth is not so keen [sharp]
   Because thou art not seen,
   Although thy breath be rude [biting]….
   (from *As You Like* It, William Shakespeare)

8. The buzz-saw snarled and rattled in the yard
   And made dust and dropped stove-length sticks of wood….
   (from "Out, out—," Robert Frost)

9. Beside the lake, beneath the trees,
    Fluttering and dancing in the breeze.…
    Ten thousand saw I at a glance
    Tossing their heads in sprightly dance.
    (from "I wandered lonely as a cloud," William Wordsworth)

Simile and metaphor

10 – 14: Indicate whether the following lines contain a simile or metaphor. Then underline the words that convey the comparison:

10. The Lord is my Shepherd; I shall not want [lack anything].
    (from Psalm 23)

11. Bent double, like old beggars under sacks,
    Knock-kneed, coughing like hags, we trudged through sludge. . .
    (from "Dulce et decorum est," Wilfred Owen)

12. I think that I shall never see
    A poem lovely as a tree. . ..
    Poems are made by fools like me,
    But only God can make a tree.
    (from "Trees," Joyce Kilmer)

13. The Lightning is a yellow fork
    from tables in the sky. . ..
    (from "The Lightning is a yellow fork," Emily Dickinson)

14. The wind was a torrent of darkness among the gusty trees,
    The moon was a ghostly galleon tossed among cloudy seas.
    (from "The Highwayman," Alfred Noyes)

Tone

15 – 17: With one adjective, identify the tone of the following lines:

15. If I were fierce, and bald, and short of breath,
    I'd live with scarlet Majors at the Base. . ..
    And when the war is done and youth stone dead,
    I'd toddle safely home and die—in bed.
    (from "Base Details," Siegfried Sassoon)

16. Break, break, break,
    At the foot of thy crags, O Sea!
    But the tender grace of a day that is dead
    Will never come back to me.
    (from "Break, break, break," Alfred, Lord Tennyson)

17. My heart is like a singing bird
    Whose nest is in a water'd shoot;
    My heart is like an apple tree
    Whose boughs are bent with thick-set fruit…
        My heart is gladder than all these
    Because my love is come to me.
    (from "A Birthday," Christina Rossetti)

18. We read one of Robert Frost's poems entitled "Out, out—" Explain how the title adds
    to the meaning of the poem.

19. In one adjective, identify the tone or attitude to life expressed in Jacques's speech in Shakespeare's play *As You Like It* that opens with these lines:

All the world's a stage,
And all the men and women merely players.
They have their exits and their entrances,
And one man in his time plays many parts,
His acts being seven ages....

20. Read this stanza from "The Bells" by Edgar Allan Poe:

Hear the sledges with the bells—
Silver bells!
What a world of merriment their melody foretells!
How they tinkle, tinkle, tinkle,
In the icy air of night!
While the stars that oversprinkle
All the heavens, seem to twinkle
With a crystalline delight;
Keeping time, time, time,
In a sort of Runic [mysterious] Rhyme,
To the tintinnabulation that so musically wells
From the bells, bells, bells, bells
Bells, bells, bells—
From the jingling and the tinkling of the bells.

Write out the words in Poe's poem that are onomatopoeic. You should list at least five words.

21. What is the mood of "The Bells"?

22. What is the implied metaphor in the following lines by Emily Dickinson?
Have passed, I thought, a Whip Lash
Unbraiding in the Sun—

When, stooping to secure it,
It wrinkled, and was gone.…

23 – 27: Choose one lyric poem we have read this year that taught you a valuable lesson or provided you with a new insight on life or human nature. In a half-page paragraph, explain in detail what you have learned by studying that particular poem.

Printed in the United States
By Bookmasters